My First Holy Communion Journey

WITH MY GUARDIAN ANGEL

Rev. Jose Kallukalam

Copyright © 2025 by Rev. Jose Kallukalam
JKbooksthatmatter Publications
Cover & Illustration Design - Jose Kallukalam
with ChatGpt & Canva assistance.
Hard Cover ISBN: ISBN: 979-8-9934189-0-2

For
First Communion
children,
with many
prayers

Invitation

Dear First Communion children,
Use this book as you prepare to receive Jesus in the Eucharist.

Dear parents and teachers,
Help the children prepare for this great event in their spiritual life.

Teacher & Parent Tips

Use this storybook for a gentle introduction to the Eucharist and First Communion. Take it slow, and enjoy the journey together.

Read one chapter at a time with your child. Take moments to pray or to discuss what you'l notice in the story.

Ask open-ended questions, such as, "What was the angel trying to say to the child?"

Repeat information with your child by recalling the book together to reinforce learning.

Explain that the child does not need to fully understand the mysteries now, but can grow in understanding through prayer and continued reception of Jesus in the Eucharist.

Chapter 1 – A Flutter of Wings

The room was quiet, but the child could not sleep.
Tomorrow was coming so quickly — the day everyone
had been talking about: First Holy Communion.
"What if I make a mistake?" the child thought.
"What if I forget what to do?"
Just then, a soft glow filled the room.

A gentle light brushed against the walls
like the flutter of wings.
"Do not be afraid," whispered a kind voice.
"I am your guardian angel.
Jesus has been waiting for this day with you.
I will walk beside you every step of the way."
The child pulled the blanket tighter,
smiled for the first time that night,
and whispered back:
"Thank you, my guardian angel."

Chapter 2 – Learning the Prayers

At catechism class,
the children practiced the Our Father.
Some voices were strong, others shy and quiet.
The child stumbled over the words
and looked down, embarrassed.

The angel leaned close and whispered:
"Every prayer is like a candle.
Some are tall, some are small,
but each one shines in God's sight.
No prayer that comes from the heart is weak."

The child lifted their head and tried again.
This time the words felt lighter,
as though they floated toward heaven.

Chapter 3 – Helping at Home

That evening, the child helped set the dinner table.
Forks and spoons clinked.
Plates were placed carefully, one by one.

The angel smiled:
"Every table reminds us of the greatest table —
the Lord's Table at Mass.
At home we share food.
At His table, Jesus shares Himself."

The child looked at the bread basket on the table
and whispered,
"Thank You, Jesus."

Chapter 4 – The First Rehearsal

The church felt big and echoing.
Children lined up to practice walking down the aisle.
The child's shoes squeaked on the polished floor.
The steps felt stiff and clumsy.

The angel whispered softly:
"Do not worry about how you walk.
Jesus is not watching your feet —
He is watching your heart."

The child smiled a little,
and on the next try,
walked with calm steps,
as if toward a friend.

Chapter 5 – A Memory of Jesus

That night, the angel told a story:
"Long ago, mothers brought
their children to Jesus.

Some thought they were too noisy, too small.
But Jesus said, 'Let the children come to me.'

He placed His hands on them and blessed them."

The child closed their eyes
and imagined being there,
safe in His arms.

A gentle peace filled their heart.

Chapter 6 – The Special Outfit

The child tried on the First Communion outfit.
It felt stiff and fancy.
The shoes pinched a little.

The angel laughed softly:
"Your clothes are lovely,
but what shines most brightly to Jesus
is your heart.
He sees love more than lace,
kindness more than cloth."

The child looked into the mirror.
For a moment,
it seemed as if a small golden light
glowed inside their chest.

Chapter 7 – The Night Before

The night before Communion,
the child felt butterflies
tumbling inside their stomach.

"What if I forget? What if I do it wrong?"

The angel drew close,
wrapping a wing gently around the child.
"Do not be afraid.
Jesus is waiting for you with love, not to test.
Your heart is enough."

The child finally drifted into sleep,
dreaming of music and light,
as the angel watched over.

Chapter 8 – The Procession Begins

The church bells rang,
and sunlight streamed through
the stained-glass windows.

Children in white lined up
to begin the procession.

The angel whispered:
"Heaven sings with you today.
Every step you take is a prayer of joy."

The child's nervousness melted into excitement
as they walked with the others toward the altar.

The altar servers led the procession,
and the pastor watched with joy.

Chapter 9 – The First Taste of Heaven

The child said aloud all the prayers of the Mass,
listened carefully to the Scripture readings,
and heard the priest's homily.

At last, the child stood before the priest.
The Host looked small,
like a simple piece of bread.
But Jesus was really present in the Host.

The angel whispered softly:
"Here is Jesus, hidden in love.
He comes to you in the simplicity of the Host,
not in crowns of gold.
Heaven itself comes to dwell in your heart."

The child received Jesus in Communion.
Warmth spread through their body,
brighter than any candle.

Chapter 10 – A Whisper of Thanks

Back in the pew, the child knelt
and closed their eyes.

"Thank You, Jesus," the child whispered.

The angel bowed beside them and said:
"Every prayer of thanks is music in Heaven.
Keep this song in your heart,
and you will never be far from Him."

The child sat very still,
listening to that song within.
And silently talked to Jesus.

Chapter 11 – The Celebration

At home, family and friends gathered.

There was a cake with candles,
balloons tied to chairs,
and laughter filling the room.

The angel whispered:
"All of this is good, but remember—
the greatest joy is Jesus in your heart.
His presence is the gift that never fades."

The child smiled, knowing this was true.

Chapter 12 – A Promise

That night, the child knelt by the bed once more.
"Thank You, Jesus, for coming into my heart today."

The angel whispered:
"Every time you receive Him,
it is like a new First Communion.

He will always be near you—
in joy and in sorrow,
in strength and in weakness.

That is why it is so important
to receive Jesus in Communion every week."

The child closed their eyes
and drifted into peaceful sleep.

Chapter 13 – Catechesis: What is the Eucharist?

The angel explained:
"Eucharist means thanksgiving.
It is the greatest gift Jesus gave us.

At the Mass the Priest prays to
God the Father,
to send the Holy Spirit upon
the bread and wine we offer on the altar.
And they become
the Body and Blood of Jesus.

We cannot see it with our eyes,
but faith tells us: Jesus is truly here.
Every time you receive Him,
you welcome His love deeper into your life."

Chapter 14 – Catechesis: Jesus at the Last Supper

The child asked:
"How do you know Jesus is in the Host?"

The angel replied: "Because He said so."

"On the night before He died,
Jesus took bread and said, 'This is my Body.'
He took the cup and said,
'This is my Blood.'
And He told His disciples,
'Do this in memory of me.'

Every Mass is that same gift of love,
given again for you."

Chapter 15 – Catechesis: The Saints' Joy

The angel whispered:
"Many saints found their greatest joy
in Holy Communion.

Saint Thérèse said
her First Communion was
the happiest day of her life.

Saint Tarcisius gave his life
to protect the Eucharist.

They remind us:
Jesus in the Eucharist is
the greatest treasure of all."

Chapter 16 – Prayer After Communion

The child asked:
"What should I do
when Jesus comes into me?"
The angel smiled:
"Thank Him, pray for your needs,
and for the needs of others."

That night, the angel prayed with the child:
"Lord Jesus,
thank You for coming into my heart today.
Stay with me always.
Help me to love You,
and to love others as You love me."

The child whispered a final word:
"Amen."

Memory Page

(Add a photo here)

On this day, _____

received First Holy Communion at _____

Parish, with Father _____

on _____

www.ingramcontent.com/pod-product-compliance
Lightning Source LLC
Chambersburg PA
CBHW051513110526
44582CB00008B/151